The Jill Kelly Poems

To Lynn:

The Jill Kelly Poems

Alessandro Porco

"It's as sweet-ass can be"

With admiration,
Alex
May 24th 2005

MISFIT

ECW PRESS

Published by ECW PRESS
2120 Queen Street East, Suite 200, Toronto, Ontario, Canada M4E IE2

NATIONAL LIBRARY OF CANADA CATALOGUING IN PUBLICATION

Porco, Alessandro
The Jill Kelly poems / Alessandro Porco.

"A MisFit book".
ISBN 1-55022-687-8

I. Title.

PS8631.073J44 2005   c811'.6   C2004-907055-X

Editor: Michael Holmes/a misFit book
Cover and Text Design: Darren Holmes
Typesetting: Mary Bowness
Printing: Marc Veilleux Imprimeur

This book is set in Goudy and Americana.

The publication of The Jill Kelly Poems has been generously
supported by the Canada Council, the Ontario Arts Council, the Ontario Media
Development Corporation, and the Government of Canada through the Book
Publishing Industry Development Program. Canadä

DISTRIBUTION
CANADA: Jaguar Book Group, 100 Armstrong Avenue, Georgetown, ON, L7G 5S4

PRINTED AND BOUND IN CANADA

ECW PRESS
ecwpress.com

Contents

The Jill Kelly Poems

The Porcoda

Acknowledgements

Some of the poems (often in different forms) have appeared in the following publications: *Autobiographia Cinematica* (above/ ground press chapbook, 2004), *Grain Magazine*, *Headlight Anthology*, *Matrix*, *N^{TH}Position*, *Pissing Ice* (Book Thug, 2004), and *Queen Street Quarterly*.

"O Canadian Ghazal" is for Alexandra Pasian and Mo. "Heat" is for Kevin Flynn.

Big ups to:

David McGimpsey, for all the beers, baseball, and brains, often at the same time; Carolyn Smart, for indulging my rants and raves about the movies (esp. all things Scorsese) and, of course, introducing me to poetry; Jon Paul Fiorentino (Tara and baby Lily, too) for your kind company; Michael Holmes and ECW for your guidance throughout the process; 4 Birch St. — Jed Devenish, Sergio Palladini, Jared Storms; the Embassy — Michael "MacT" Mactaggart, Geoff Morrison, Ed Shin; and the Begleys, Jason Camlot, Angali Chakraborty, Shanna Cipressi, Mary di Michele, Kevin Flynn, the Groes, Judith Herz, Jill Kelly, Moberley Luger, Eva Moran, Alexandra Pasian, Olivia Rotheram, Yaël Schlick, and Moez Surani.

And, of course, love and thanks to my extraordinarily funny and talented sisters, Jennifer and Sabrina; Mauro and Marie up in Barrie — for the beers and meals; and the always supportive mom and dad.

I write of youth, of love, and have access
By these to sing of cleanly wantonness.
I sing of dews, of rains, and piece by piece,
Of balm, of oil, of spice, and ambergris.
I sing of times trans-shifting, and I write
How roses first came red and lilies white.
I write of groves, of twilight, and I sing
The court of Mab and of the fairy king.

— Robert Herrick

for my Family and Friends

BAD BOYS

THE REAL G

A self-proclaimed brother
who'd smother your mother as soon as he finished
backside sliding into your little sister,
the one they call Eazy never went in for
PG rated big-pimpin' or gettin' jiggy,
& if he were alive today,
he'd hard-knock life Jay-Z back to reality
& send Big Willy's willy styles back to west Philly.

At L.A.'s Mount Sinai,
E's pneumonic-induced fever arrested the logic
once distinguishing him from mass suckers,
making it impossible to drop rhymes for seven kids
from six mothers. He lay stock still, emaciated;
Tomika breast-feeding their new-born
in the bullet-proof shadow of twin big-boi Samoans
standing guard over his death-bed like totems.

Lawyers bowdlerized his last werdz, excising
every *mother*-expletive for reporters;
but defiant to the end, he refused to wear
the regulation hospital-blue gown. Rigged-up
in Raider gear instead, activator proud
with the So-Cal jheri-curl, I like to think Eazy
met Death as only Eazy could, that ruthless
motherfuckin' squeal we all came to love
in fully-loaded motherfuckin' G-effect:
"What up, Dawg? Original Mista 1-8-7 —
it's about time. It's about motherfuckin' time."
They'd compare weapons —
sawed-off vs. scythe —
& bump, hydraulically, towards the light.

ODE TO CHRISTINA AGUILERA

In Miami, she sluts about South Beach, keepin' it real
    Coppin' feels
Of tranies, queens, & Creatine beefs, *latina* roots
    & fuck-me boots
Moving her to salsa-sweat the dirrty-night away
    With clearly gay
Muchachos queer-eyed blind to her hip-shakes & dips
    Mid Cosmo sips —

To the 24-hour piercing parlor off the strip, where,
    On a dare,
Our *muy caliente Mammita* of Pop unzips to her muff;
    A lit splif
Calms liquored nerves on ORANGE alert as Mr. Skull-
    Bones holds the needle
Set to go where many-a-men have gone before,
    Inking *muncho mi amor* —

You complete me, Christina, like a genie in a bottle
    — Like a full-
Blown case of the clap in your lap — Doctor's order:
    Come on over!

I'M READY, COACH . . . PUT ME IN

Being beautiful's like playing quarterback
for the Fighting Irish of Notre Dame:
every home-game Saturday's a sell-out
in South Bend, IN, & from sideline to sideline,
up through the grandstand nose-bleeds,
all eyes are on you, kid, strutting your all-
American stuff over to the fifty-yard line
for the coin-toss: *call it in the air* —
                              my name's Rudy,
the practice squad's tackle-dummy, bull's-eyed
between the numbers; I haul ass at the mill,
dreaming up one final down where, with some
Gipper luck, I score a taste of the good life &
convert my fivefootnothing onehundrednothing
into something — *play like a champion today.*

THE BLAME GAME

Blame it on funkyspunk
Blame it on drunkmonks
Blame it on the bull and the bunk
And the funk on a nastydunk
Just leave me out of it!

Blame it on the cupidity of ibid
Blame it on Rorschach kismet
Blame it on the mysteries of an id
Ancient and wild like the horns of an ibex
Just leave me out of it!

Blame it on defective rubbers
Blame it on the cream of cucumbers
Blame it on heavy-metal drummers
Who dream of supercalifragilistic slumbers
Just leave me out of it!

Blame it on the mutton pong of lamb
Blame the hoodlums who love on the lam
The gubernatorial candidate dancing a cancan
— But not his Bourbon St. Madam —
Oh, and leave me out of it!

Blame it on a thousand shades of blue
Blame it on Kung-Faux Kung-Fu
Blame it on the imminent rhyme of *couscous*
Blame it on — what's the use?
Just leave me the hell out of it!

MY BOYFRIEND'S OBSESSED WITH LARRY BIRD, & I'M OBSESSED WITH ROMANCE

a spring break sonnet, after Dan Patrick

"What's a girl to do in French Lick, IN? —
sip twist-cap strawberry wine from a swirly-straw
pool-side on a next-exit motel chaise-longue,
long far gone from an ocean of umbrella drinks & beer-

bongs, frat-boys slipping tube-tops as flimsy as thongs
off sorority pledges desperate to soothe
the deep-bone bruises of last night's mechanical bull-rides
by simply floating away today; every jolt & jerk-

off in the distance, dwindling like a cruise-liner:
its Captain, dashing at ship's helm
— a blond, buff, nautical Bjorn — in a crisp white decorated uniform,

sets course for where I am, arrangements made
to save a flotsam babe as the fantasy demands: rescue-
flare embers lighting my body like a motel billboard?"

THE SOUNDTRACK TO SEX — VOL. 1

Nino Rotta's *Love Theme from The Godfather* 🌼 Westside Grip

Kelly Ripa laugh-loop 🌼 Squashing the Deckchair

Dennis Miller's *Citizen Arcane* 🌼 Fisting Slings

Ann Coulter vs. Katie Couric (Wed. June 26, 2002 on NBC) 🌼 69

The O.J. Verdict 🌼 Black Bee

Jezebelle Bond in *Vixxen & The Return of Vixxen* 🌼 Cowgirl

Malcolm X's Harvard Lectures 🌼 Angry Dragon

Real Madrid 4 vs. Juventus 3 (Spanish broadcast) 🌼 The Walrus

Tap dancing 🌼 DVDA (Double-vaginal-double-anal)

The Scorpions' *Wind of Change* 🌼 Wobbly H

Al Jazeera TV 🌼 Davey Crockett

Monday Night Football with Al Michaels & John Madden 🌼 Leapfrog

Scorsese's *Goodfellas* 🌼 Reverse Piggy-back

I SCREAM, YOU SCREAM, WE ALL SCREAM FOR *CIALIS*

Pussy farts turn the stiffest stiffy
   Soft as soft ice-cream;
And no matter how many licks, if
I hear pussy farts, my stiffest
Stiffy is nothing but drips, to lift
   My melted but a wet, sticky dream —
Pussy farts turn the stiffest stiffy
   Soft as soft ice-cream.

THE LONELY STREET OF DREAMS

One Night Only. Ten bucks a pop.
My guitar hero, Reb Beach, live at *Hot Rocks*.
This is it, I thought, the start
of the instrumental guitar-rock revival.
Only thirteen years old, a friend
of my oldest brother bounced the door;
Dude hooked up the ticket,
he snuck me in.
Leather chaps, tassels, studded hat —
Reb sweet-talked, trash-talked,
played possum with
his 7-string Jem-model Ibanez
like she was a Tijuana whore, Senorita Inez,
her bangedandbattered mahogany
body, by the pluck of a thousand picks,
singing a thousand notes of sin:
24-fret pinch harmonics,
whammy-bar dive-bombs,
eight-finger tap-dancing,
light-speed speed-picking weaving
its way over jazz-inflected
prog-rock changes — ex-*Winger* lead-
man, 7-string-slinger
— you name it, he did it, & I witnessed it
from start to finish.
                        After the gig,
Reb answered shop-talk questions,
signed autographs,
passed out monogrammed picks
for the gathered crowd
of guitarshop woodshed shredheads
(myself included)
who lived to steal his every lick
under the impression that doing so
would help us score chicks;

what Reb didn't do —
unlike some *to remain un-named* guitar heroes I know (Nikki Sixx)
— is slip backstage to disrespect his Jem
by jamming it neck-deep
into the nipsy-end of the mother end
of a cougar-daughter tag-team.

Well, the instrumental-rock revival didn't take
(bus shelters, food courts, bathroom
walls, stalls, smalls
of teenage backs
— to my disappointment, no
I love THE DIXIE DREGS graffiti, or
RACER X RULES tattoos),
though something infinitely more important did:
waitresses
uniformed in baby-sized baby-Ts,
florescent bar-logos pressed across their chests:
remember, at thirteen,
the closest I'd ever been to the real-life stuff
of big jugs was scrambled porn
— even then I couldn't say for sure.
And now, One Night Only's
a lifetime spent; I've paid & I've paid
& I've paid the price
of admission,
I admit; & looking at you,
all's I can think is,
"Here I go again,
15% & my heart's the tip."

MÉNAGE À BUSH TWINS

a cento composed of ESPN Sportscenter anchor catchphrases

Good wood,
solid spank, major league
crank. Like gravy
on a biscuit, it's all good.

That's a double play,
if you're scoring at home . . . or
if your're scoring by your-
self. Dare I say —

Barbara, Jenna, the First twins —
en fuego?
I'm not sure if I know
what the pitch is, but it tastes like chicken.

This just in: Bush is good, jelly
to the donut, baby! — Let it three.

MACGUFFIN

"What's that package?" asked the first man.
"Oh, that's a MacGuffin," replied his companion.
"What's a MacGuffin?"
"It's an apparatus for trapping lions in the Scottish highlands."
"But there are no lions in the Scottish highlands."
"Then that's no MacGuffin."
                    — Angus MacPhail, of the London Film Society (1939)

The sign says NO EXIT, & I am lost without you.
Turks ride bareback across the horizon,
armed with dzeferdars, kuburas & yataghans.

In the glove compartment, there's a starter's pistol
& a blue key. The key unlocks the box. Inside
you'll find a bouquet of Anatolian cyclamen

without a card & your severed thumb, up
from the depths to break the surface tranquility
of our pretty lake, to hitch a lift into the plot.

The radio's playing our song, the detective
would like a word, but our horse has just arrived
& there's a war to prepare for. I tether our

thoroughbred to the steering-wheel, & we make love
in the trunk as he trots us into battle. If captured
& asked "Who is the man in the wheelchair?"

tell them everything, tell them nothing —

WHEN I QUIT MULLING OVER A HISTORY
OF WORDS WITH SILENT LETTERS,
SHE LAYS BESIDE ME IN THE DAWN OF TIME,
PETRIFIED, LIKE A

pterodactyl

RAMBO: FIRST LOVE

"Out of the aether,
into the jungle of my heart,
where no soldier

since has touched-
down in one piece, as the quick
of my grip to such

impious feet
is eclipsed only by the quick
of my machete

lopping them off — his
orders were to complete aerial
reconnaissance,

not engage the
enemy."

ODE TO BALZAC

Don't let the title fool you —
truth be told, should this Ode's proposed subject ever
come up, say, in a FRENCH LITERATURE
Final Jeopardy, for example, the answer-clue

given contestants would be utterly lost on me;
or, too, if in the company of *literati*,
who, let it be said, insert foreign appellations of literary
reputation into dinner-party

conversations to prove their intellectual ballast —
like pompadour coiffures; tweed jackets with elbow patches;
super-grandiloquence (cf. "appellations"); & handlebar moustaches —
I just get a kick out of saying Balzac,

emphasis on
the homophonic *entendre*. Ball. Sack. Perhaps juvenile,
but like I said, I like it said: my title's
a smokescreen, a MacGuffin, man without country, poem
    without subject —

"There are no lions in the highlands of Scotland!"
The aphorism delimits a theory of suspense put forth by Hitchcock —
it would be a shame not to . . . Hitch. *Cock.*
— where style is visible substance, some invisible hand

pens *The End* in elegant cursive, but
by then no lesson's learned — crisis averted — no moral
    imperative imparted:
escapist entertainment, or have I created art
for art's sack, like *The Life & Times of B.J. King* by Tugnutt?

GOOD WILL HUNTING FOR BEAVER

"My boy'z z'wicket smawt!" —
　Smooth as a Larry Bird jump-shot
Discussing epidemic small-pox
　In colonial America; the Red Sox–

Yankee rivalry; or chasing Irish-Catholic
　Kilts, hike-pinned high to pink
Upper-thigh heights, 2 inches above nun-cut
　Regulation, ½ inch below their !@#$%

ELEGY

Depression's too much; more malaise, or
What people are in the habit of calling a funk —
Wake late; if I can muster the oomph,
Masturbate; take a second or two, weigh
Pros and cons of a hot shower, clean shave —
Why not save 'em for another day? So,
I do; and that's me, fit company for a skunk.
Till you show, baby, all twinkle twinkle
— Burning hot, head first, you burst, a ball
Of fire — how I wonder what you are!
With a kiss, you took the stink from my days
And light, O, love, set my crotch ablaze:
     To hell with whatever band of the zodiac
     You've gone awol from, I need you more.

ECW PRESS

I Should Never Have Fired the Sentinel

Jennifer LoveGrove

LoveGrove uses language
like a mad scientist....
— Lynn Crosbie

A daring...downright
smutty collection....
— Josey Vogels

Alessandro Porco

The Jill Kelly Poems

ECW Press

THE SOUNDTRACK TO SEX — VOL. 2

Christian Bök reading Hugo Ball ❧ Bukkake

Metallica's *For Whom the Bell Tolls-Fade to Black* ❧ Donkey Punch

An eighteen-wheeler in reverse ❧ Shrimping

Toby Keith's *Who's Your Daddy?* ❧ Persuading the Debtor

An espresso machine ❧ Shop Vac

Ezra Pound *Live from Rapallo* box-set ❧ The Wheelbarrow

The Cuckoo-clock monologue ❧ Spit Roast

Dylan Thomas reading "Do Not Go Gently Into That Good Night" ❧ Shirley Temple

Dubai Aviational School Control Tower ❧ The Zombie Mask

Celine Dion's *All By Myself* ❧ Bullwinkle

James Carville vs. Tucker Carlson ❧ Reverse Cowgirl

Oliver Stone's *Platoon* ❧ Shocker

Britney Spears crying during an interview with Diane Sawyer ❧ Daisy Chain

RAISON D'ÊTRE

This poem includes the word somnambulist
    Because I like the way it sounds.
There's no meaning to be derived by formalists.
Why not include the word somnambulist?
It's so damn oblivious. I consulted my linguist,
    And Dr. So-Shu assures me I'm allowed
To include my *mot juste* somnambulist
    Wherever, whenever: my ear's mind's sound.

23 HAIKU

Hail Muse! & so on & so forth; I've said what I set out to say,
   filled my quota for the day

"Let me look into my crystal ball" — life as a duck at the table
   of a quack

One thing is just as likely another, so why bother with these
   silly games?

Lost in translation is *we're gonna be alright*

Always use the active voice, except in the cases of bank robbers
   & mad scientists, glory hogs the lot of them to begin with —

"The plan was perfect," famous last words of famous last words

— and that's how it happened, Joe, like a steaming cup

Please leave a message after the tone

According to so & so is a poor way to begin anything other than
   a friendship

"The zaftig JAP surprise attacked the young man's banana
   hammock," or is that just what the government wants you
   to believe?

Hola she said, though having never been to Spain, and with
   clouds like lampshades around the sun

. . . like French Toast, it's the condition (Audi) not the
   situation (Pavarotti) that matters most

Tonight it's for the best — when is it ever not?

A turn for the worse, the snap-drop of an elevator well-past capacity: Poesie, what have you done fore me lately?

On your twenty-first birthday, Sis, forget to empty your pockets

If what the stars are saying is true, I'd avoid me too

We left it unsaid, determined to not let it ruin our breakfast: the most important meal of the day

There was a mess followed by dinner & dance, your ordinary happy wedding

A *randomness, a darkness of one's own* sent me on my way

Unlucky thirteen! After but one kiss, Laura's vanished into the fore of my lyrics every since

Hair, as thin as the air at the tips of mile-high mountains

The baedecker says, "There are things to do in Denver when you're dead," but love is not one of them

If distance makes love understandable, I'm a long-ways away with no intention of returning

KING KONG'S SONNET

Mission control orders its
fly-boys to riddle Kong with heat-seeking missiles;
he plummets

to the street, sepsis
sets in, groans explode from his throat like flak,
then, nothing . . . silence.

Dwan wept, wiped her tears
on Kong's hide; I figure it's but a matter of time
before she cries for

a warm shoulder to cry on:
that's my cue to swoop — if routine rejection's
taught me anything, one

shoulder's as good as another. Why not mine? —
Baby, it's evolution.

ODE TO MARIA SHARAPOVA

Rain-delayed at Roland-Garros,
we tumble, we tussle about the wet clay-courts,
  amorous combatants in prelapserian sport
    — the fever breaks, I wake. Diagnosis: Mononucleosis.

Oh, to be sick always, again & again!
Overcast Wimbledon's our chance to tube to Piccadilly,
  find an American sports-bar, get silly-
    drunk on belly-shots, hump, & name our love-child ESPN.

The fickle sun of England rises for tea-
biscuits & clotted cream, its oath on this final Saturday,
  "a champion's effort (one ray at a time)," blazing
    — dare I say, *en fuego?* — but it's you, Maria,

hoisting the Venus Rosewater Dish, only seventeen years of age.
Is whatever early promise I did possess (if any) lost,
  nothing more than a service toss
    the wind got hold of & launched into space?

Does the grounding reality of gravity qualify as a regret?
The *Get Well Soon* balloons
  that once enlivened the hospital room
    droop like old-lady breasts

(gravity, once again), & it's a sign
  — upon which I'm meant to cast a disparaging eye —
    the moon's as likely as my ball to fall from the sky,
      & everyone's born to lose . . . except for tall drinks of Russian.

O CANADIAN GHAZAL

And the funny thing is it knows we know
About it and still wants us to go on believing
In what it so unskillfully imitates . . .
                                    — John Ashbery

I

As wise as the old trees
Would have you believe they are —

II

A young widow by trade,
Ut Pictura Poesis is my maiden name.

III

But when you wake up to the
Wrong kind of insurance, what then?

AUTOBIOGRAPHIA LITERARIA AS A THREE-MINUTE SHORT FILM

0:00 – 1:00

When I was a child
I hated this & hated that
& thought life so tough: thumb-
sucking complaints.

*

1:00 – 2:00

But audiences need
action: include a one-time
deal gone sour, & then jump-cut
forward to

*

2:00 – 3:00

present day. There's
a girl I've met; she takes
pleasure in my lies of omission.
Imagine!

THE JILL KELLY
POEMS

Tityre, tu patulae recubans sub tegmine fagi
siluestrem tenui Musam meditaris auena;
nos patriae finis et dulcia linquimus arua.
Nos patriam fugimus; tu, Tityre, lentus in umbra
formosam resonare doces Amaryllida siluas.

— Virgil

I care not for these ladies that must be wooed and prayed.
Give me kind Amaryllis, the wanton country maid.
Nature art disdaineth; her beauty is her own.
Who when we court and kiss, she cries "Forsooth, let go!"
But when we come where comfort is, she never will say no.

— Thomas Campion

But Love has pitched his mansion in
The place of excrement;
For nothing can be sole or whole
That has not been rent.

— William Butler Yeats

JILL KELLY'S ARS POETICA

Breakfast in bed & down on all fours,
You're eggs-over-easy, munchin' for more;
Vegans protest & brand it obscene,
But there's no starving my anal queen.

Working-class to the bone, I love my porn,
& at minimum wage it's all I can afford;
Marxists can lecture & label it obscene,
But they can't put a price on my anal queen.

No clean-cut air-brushed auto-shop pin-up:
It's dirt-box zoom-ins & spunk on a C-cup;
Puritans can preach & declare it obscene,
But I still love you, my anal queen.

JILL KELLY CONDUCTS RESEARCH INTO THE MOST NOTORIOUS BLACKBEARD'S MOST NOTORIOUS WIVES, MOST NOTABLY ABSENT FROM DANIEL DEFOE'S MOST ENTERTAINING *PIRATES*

Fact: the thong dates back
To wife number four, one-time
Carolina seamstress wooed
By the Cap's sack & jack.

She dipped in the sloop's
Eye-patch stash, stitched three
Strips of deck rope *et voilà*
Hidden jewels & booty to boot.

We frig, we fiddle, we swallow & spit
Yo ho! A gang-bang on the seas;
We bend & bone every mate on the ship
Yo ho! A pirate's-wife life for me.

Studies of early 17th century fashion
Fail to note that the busk,
Originally made of iron, wood,
& later, whalebone,

Slotted in basque fronts, was
Discarded by wife ten & replaced
With an early model butt-plug
Cut in the shape of a blunderbuss.

We gulp, we plug, we jack & strap
Yo ho! A gang-bang on the seas;
We ball the cannons blasting our gaps
Yo ho! A pirate's-wife life for me.

Kink, anyone?
The cat-o'-nine-tales, a flogging device
Wife number eight asked
Be whacked on the chubb of her bum

Till sweet coo-juice
As intoxicating as west-Indie rum
Gushed from the keg
Tapped between her legs.

We drop & drool, we jump & jiggle
Yo ho! A gang-bang on the seas;
For trolling our story, thank you Jill
Yo ho! A pirate's-wife life for me.

JILL KELLY'S GERTRUDE STEIN

A boob is a boob is a boob is a boob is a boob is a.

JILL KELLY'S TITTY-BOP SONNET

What's to stop me, say, from writing
 A beauty's-best blazon, never looking
Above, below, or beyond gianormous
 Jugs jugging-in at a C-cup 36?

Well, sure, some critic might claim,
 Porco è porcu, his pen unable to sustain
A poetic argument of "real" value;
 But that's no reason not to do as I do,

Which is express a love of bib-bubs
 In a fourteen-line song to the God of
Titty-bops — *hast thou forsaken me?*
 Why not hand over a naked Jill Kelly

So as I can finally stop writing this
 Thing & slide my this between her thats?

JILL KELLY'S DELIGHT IN DISORDER

Typical monthly-mag spreads
pretty much go something like this:
easily identifiable location
(mountain-side; limo; Mexican restaurant),
its apropos costumes
(backpack-stiletto; corsage-stiletto;
sombrero-stiletto-taco supreme combo *por favor*),
followed by the obligatory
one-page peeler, then finally a spread 'em
that puts the spread in spreads.
This one should've been no different.
Jill's orange-in-a-can tan sets itself
against a symmetrical off-white crotch line;
blond crop-banged locks:
not one split-end or root to report.
She's decided on a pastoral scene;
good call. Bottle of white wine,
white linens, a white long-dong dildo,
green bottled slip-&-slide
lube-icide, & a basket filled with
the very things the Sisters of Sacred Heart
once filled baskets with on picnics.
They detail the ever-green knoll
that straddles her in the background.
Kudos, M. Des Sets.
It's perfect — as if the waters of some river
somewhere nearby are flowing
& I could hear the leap of its goodly fish
in delight: the world's alright —
                                        perfect

but for your right foot, Jill,
kicking at the screen, wanting
out as much as I want in: its big toe
4x the size of your one bared
nipple, a nipple I hardly even notice
on account of its disproportion:
an anomaly so bizarre is that podiatric wreck
the crucifix around your neck
slipped by me till this very moment
— *mmmmm!* to suck on your
big catholic porno toe,
which doth bewitch me more than when art
is too precise in every part
— or, rather, A-*mmmmm*-en!

I'M DREAMING OF A JILL KELLY PRODUCTIONS CHRISTMAS SPECIAL

JEZEBELLE BOND:	I got the South for your North pole
(Chorus)	*Fuck me, Santa! Fuck me, Santa!*
TYLER FAITH:	Bam the Al *a la* Cal in my Alabama hole
(Chorus)	*Fuck me, Santa! Fuck me, Santa!*

MONICA MAYHEM:	Not too big, not too small — just like Goldiloxxx
(Chorus)	*Fuck me, Santa! Fuck me, Santa!*
ALEXIS AMORE:	Your "just right" cock in my gift-wrapped boxxx
(Chorus)	*Fuck me, Santa! Fuck me, Santa!*

JENNA HAZE:	Before we do the nookie, eat my cookie
(Chorus)	*Fuck me, Santa! Fuck me, Santa!*
SUMMER CUMMINGS:	And I'll drinkum your jizzum like milkum
(Chorus)	*Fuck me, Santa! Fuck me, Santa!*

JILL KELLY'S THE GIRL NEXT DOOR

The girl next door's a porn-star,
   Her picket-fence as white as a facial.
I spend weekends washing my car
Because the girl next door's a porn-star,
And a good neighbour knows water
   And soap mix a make-shift lube for anal;
And though by no means a porn-star,
   I too fuck ass and give facials.

JILL KELLY PRODUCTIONS'
LEAGUE OF EXTRAORDINARY WOMEN

First, Jezebelle Bond, or, as I like to call her,
the Literary one. The most learned of all
adopted industry names: Ian Fleming
meets Baal sex-cult worshipper.

"Double O Ho" (as she's referred to
by subscription types) only recently decided
to break out of the girl-girl scene
& into the man show.

Next up, the "other" Jenna — that is, Miss Haze;
every part of her sickly frame making up
for a fresh-off-the-bus, bad career-name decision,
which could have ended it all, another

lost pup to be picked up by a Pierce Patchett chump.
It's made her hit the gym harder. A cock-
ring brawler in the bod of a blood-starved vamp
nowadays; meet Porno's Mina Harker.

& of course, Jill's every eye lights the sky
when talk comes round to *the* Haven:
a one-word two-syllable three-hole slice of
suck-*ee* suck-*ee* heaven. Haven

studies the shaolin way & two-gun pump
mastered by Chow Yun Fat in hopes of crossing
into action-heroine mainstream in cineplexes
from Portland, Maine to Portland, Oregon.

Jezebelle, Jenna, & Haven:
together, they are JKProductions'
League of Extraordinary Women, fighting
crime in the year of our Lord 2005.

JILL KELLY'S TWIDDLE DA TWAT

Twiddle me doo
Twiddle me dumb
Twiddle my twat
Pluggle my bum

Twiddle me this
Twiddle me that
Twiddle my twat
Pluggle my spot

Scuttle me buttle
Piddle me paddle
Tickle my piggle
Twattle my twiddle

JILL KELLY'S RETIREMENTO SENTIMENTO CENTO

The material contained herein includes
Fingers, thumbs, tongues, & spooge
A girl who doesn't like wearing clothes
Opened to accept the smooth probe

The Pro+Plus pill enlarges your penis
Stick your dick where my finger is
Yes, most women agree size does matter
The Mr. Satisfier satisfies every desire

Order *Doin' The Babysitter* for $4.95
Receive your free copy of *Fat Girls Try*
Order the *My Best Friend's Gramma* Trilogy
We guarantee 100% shipping privacy

JILL KELLY'S ANAL PHILOLOGY

Bullet-hole.
That's one I'd never heard before,
& I fancy myself
a connoisseur of a more sordid sort than most
when it pertains to anything
back-door related.
So, naturally — or, unnaturally,
depending on your view of things
— the expression would be
something like
shooting the bullet-hole.
Simple. I like it. I mean, it's no
painting the dirtbox
flying the red-eye
driving the Hershey highway
plowing the cornhole
or *earning your chocolate wings*
— darlings of xxx lingo —
& maybe it's a bit too action-hero,
a bit too John Woo;
nonetheless it's one more for the collection.
The thing is (to be honest)
I don't quite get it;
I guess that's what makes it poetry:
sweet-ass language all the sweet-ass time
all up in your sweet-ass pucker,
the dream of a sweet-ass lifetime come true.
Ah, but then, what is sweet-ass truth?
It's as sweet-ass can be —

THE PORCODA

'U porcu, quandu è porcu pe natura, non vala
si li fai lu strica e lava.

— Calabrese Proverb

for Olivia

MY SWEETEST BI-CURIOUS

after Catullus

My sweetest Bi-curious, live and love
Without reprove, and like a dove
Fly, fly high, soar, though to survive,
On occasion, you must muff-dive
To feed on the finest carrion spread
Between your sweetest Bi-curious girlfriend's
Legs; and when death my life doth seal
With a kiss, let my final vision be
You, my sweetest, enjoying a timely meal.
Thus, a happy bird-watcher dies happily
— White sheet draped over my head,
I'm not alive; waist-down, I'm not dead.
   The hearse carts a stiff past the cemetery gates,
   One eye on the Lord, one eye on your plate.

MY FIRST TIME; OR,
RODEO LOVE AT *RANCHMAN'S*

as seen on the W-Network's My First Time

"I lost my virginity to a mechanical bull
   Who went by the name of Squirt Gun;
Ladies, I remember: one joggle, one jiggle,
And my virginity was gone — that there's no bull!
I wish it had been slower, tender, beautiful;
   But my quarter was up and the ride was done
Before I could yelp, 'Yee-haw!' My bull —
   Poor fella — couldn't help squirtin' his gun."

A DRINKING SONG

after William Butler Yeats

Beer comes in at the mouth,
    Love comes smooth with lube,
Chicks with dicks are dudes,
    That's all you need know is truth.

THOUGH I'D LIKE TO EXPLAIN
THE FINER POINTS OF IT ALL TO YOU

It's not as if we are dealing with the complex uses of a new metal

THANK YOU FATHERS FOR YOUR DAUGHTERS

after Sappho

First
the moon,
then
the Pleiades
go down

       . . .] Hey,
you know
what I really dig
is
when chicks
go down

on each other [. . .

. . .] sometimes
the moon is just the moon,
the stars the stars,

Oh
the porn stars [. . .

SOLARIUM

after Salvatore Quasimodo

A tectonic shift
Broke the heart of the Earth
Like a back — disks
Slip, ring weighs on ring, the
Cartilaginous sting
As blinding as the Sun,
And, suddenly it is evening.

BRAGGADOCHIO, SKIPPY

The zig-zag nights pass spoonfuls of peanut-butter at a time,
& I swear on my walk-in-closet life
CBS news' LIVE FROM KABUL Lara Logan's licking her lips at me
    through the TV:

anti-war demonstrators try to nut-sack that dream (at least)
    once a week.
"War . . . what is it good for?" they chant;
uh, super-model military-correspondents — that's what!

I really do believe in liberal democracy, so Birkenstock stomp
all you want from Atwater to St. Denis;
but make-believe foreplay & sandwich jelly are worth every
    casualty.

There's no reason to worry how cowardly I'd be on the front line,
& to imagine how I might not be
way too much poetry for my medically-exempt heart.

HEAT

Archie Lampman on spring break

Beyond me on the sand the sun
    Soaks on *Girls Gone Wild* bottoms,
I count the margaritas one by one
    Every other double-downed in rum;

In the shadow of my sombrero
    All thoughts grow dull and blurry,
One parting shot of *Jose Cuervo*
    For the courage to "go ugly early."

TO BE CARVED ON A WALL AT LEONARD HALL, QUEEN'S UNIVERSITY

Long ago, here, I, poet Alessandro Porco,
The Chronic blaring, blazed the bionic till loco
Then munched on Twinkies and Ho Hos
As Dre and Snoop warned "Bitches ain't shit but Hos
And tricks"; and I chased shots of So-Co
With shots of So-Co for the liquid-courage to slump-bust Hippos
I tranqued SAFARI NIGHT at *The Cocomo*;
And through it all found time to read Pound's Li-Po
— "The willow flakes falling like snow" —
But despised the hermetic difficulty of Po-Mo,
Its corresponding theoretical lingo
Making as much sense to me as barking dingoes;
And found time for steaming cups of Joe,
The song-birds singing Spring; while Winter's spiked hot cocoa
Sent my romantic head reeling like a Yo-Yo;
And on the Common, or on the shore of Lake Ontario,
A faux-Lampman basking in the sun's glow
Upon sowing my wildest oats —
Freshman freaks "experimenting" with deaky choke-
Holds so fierce they knocked me out cold,
More often than not before I'd even shot my load,
Leaving my balls as blue as Pluto —
I contemplated a future as arbitrary as the logos,
A future so sublime, I had no desire to let my beautiful youth go
The way, not of the Golden Gael but, of the Dodo:
(Queen's college colours we are wearing once again)
May your time here be as well spent as mine,
(Soiled as they are by the battle and the rain)
May your time here be as described in these lines,
(Yet another victory to wipe away the stain)
And not four years riding J-DUC Centre pines,
(So, Gaels go in and win!)
Not four years on Richardson Stadium's side-lines:
What's the sport of Kings? Queens, Queens, Queens . . .

DOGGY STYLE

Thirsty bitch, she laps up the Schnapps
in her glass in a snap, *a snap* —
and that's how she loves, too! No time
for play in the park: chasing wood
sticks, chomping bones — as good as Time
chomping its own wings. No; one
trick pawflip of the light switch and,
from there on in, it's all business:

hindlegs and haunches up in the dark,
tails and tongues awag as we shag, but
not the slightest bite mark to boast of
on my morning walk; not even the echo of
— *ruff, ruff* — the bitch's bark: leaving me
to my thoughts, in silence, licking my nuts.